First World War
and Army of Occupation
War Diary
France, Belgium and Germany

58 DIVISION
Divisional Troops
290 Brigade Royal Field Artillery
20 January 1917 - 8 March 1919

WO95/2995/3

The Naval & Military Press Ltd
www.nmarchive.com
Published in association with The National Archives

Published by

The Naval & Military Press Ltd

Unit 10 Ridgewood Industrial Park,
Uckfield, East Sussex,
TN22 5QE England
Tel: +44 (0) 1825 749494

www.naval-military-press.com
www.nmarchive.com

This diary has been reprinted in facsimile from the original. Any imperfections are inevitably reproduced and the quality may fall short of modern type and cartographic standards.

Contents

Document type	Place/Title	Date From	Date To
Heading	WO95/2995-2		
Heading	B E F 58 Division Troops 290 Brigade R F A 1917 Jan-1919 Mar		
Heading	War Diary Of 290 Bde R F A 1917 January		
War Diary	Heytesbury	20/01/1917	20/01/1917
War Diary	Havre	22/01/1917	22/01/1917
War Diary	Occoches	28/01/1917	28/01/1917
War Diary	Noeux	05/02/1917	05/02/1917
War Diary	Lucheux	06/02/1917	06/02/1917
War Diary	Heytesbury	20/01/1917	20/01/1917
War Diary	Havre	22/01/1917	22/01/1917
War Diary	Occoches	28/01/1917	28/01/1917
War Diary	Noeux	05/02/1917	05/02/1917
War Diary	Lucheux	06/02/1917	06/02/1917
War Diary	Heytesbury	20/01/1917	20/01/1917
War Diary	Havre	22/01/1917	22/01/1917
War Diary	Occoches	28/02/1917	28/02/1917
War Diary	Noeux	05/02/1917	05/02/1917
War Diary	Lucheux	07/02/1917	07/02/1917
War Diary	Lucheux	24/02/1917	24/02/1917
War Diary	Le Cauchie	17/03/1917	28/03/1917
War Diary	Boiry St Rictrude	31/03/1917	13/04/1917
War Diary	B 17b 3 6	14/04/1917	22/04/1917
Heading	War Diary Of 290th Bde R.F.A. From 3/5/17 To 28/5/17		
War Diary	B.17.B.3 6	03/05/1917	17/05/1917
War Diary	War Diary Of 290 Bde R F A		
War Diary	B 12d 15 85	20/01/1917	20/01/1917
War Diary	B 17.b. 3 6	24/06/1917	26/07/1917
War Diary	Ytres	02/08/1917	05/08/1917
War Diary	Heninel	20/08/1917	21/08/1917
War Diary	Beaurains	26/08/1917	03/09/1917
War Diary	Herzeele	06/09/1917	07/09/1917
War Diary	I.1.a	14/09/1917	14/09/1917
War Diary	Wilsons Farm	19/09/1917	23/10/1917
War Diary	Cheddar Villa	31/10/1917	13/11/1917
Miscellaneous	D A G 3rd Echelon Base	31/12/1917	31/12/1917
War Diary	Estree Area	04/12/1917	17/12/1917
War Diary	Cane Post	12/01/1918	28/02/1918
War Diary	In The Field	01/03/1918	31/03/1918
Heading	Headquarters 290th Brigade R.F.A. April 1918		
War Diary		01/04/1918	29/07/1918
Heading	290th Brigade R F A August 1918		
War Diary		31/07/1918	30/11/1918
War Diary	Quevaucamps	01/12/1918	08/03/1919

BEF

58 DIVISION TROOPS

290 BRIGADE RFA

(FORMERLY 2/1 LONDON BDE)

1917 JAN — 1919 MAR

Box 2995

Vol 1 # 2 58
43

WAR DIARY

OF

290 BDE RFA.

1917 JANUARY

290th Bde R.F.A.

Instructions regarding War Diaries and Intelligence Summaries are contained in F. S. Regs., Part II. and the Staff Manual respectively. Title pages will be prepared in manuscript.

WAR DIARY
or
INTELLIGENCE SUMMARY.
(Erase heading not required.)

Army Form C. 2118.

Place	Date	Hour	Summary of Events and Information	Remarks and references to Appendices
Shaftesbury	20/1/17	10/pm	Brigade left Southampton for France.	
Havre	23/1/17	10 pm.	Left Havre 22/1/17 for Auxi-le-Chateau & billeted at OCCOCHES	
Occoches	28/1/17	1 pm	Occupied Billets at NOEUX.	
Noeux	5/2/17	11 am	Occupied Billets at LUCHEUX.	
Lucheux	6/2/17	–	"D" Battery converted into a 6 gun Battery.	

[illegible] Lt Colonel
Comdg 290th Bde R.F.A.

24/2/17

T2134. Wt. W708—776. 500000. 4/15. Sir J. C. & S.

Instructions regarding War Diaries and Intelligence Summaries are contained in F. S. Regs., Part II. and the Staff Manual respectively. Title pages will be prepared in manuscript.

WAR DIARY
or
INTELLIGENCE SUMMARY.
(Erase heading not required.)

Army Form C. 2118.

Place	Date	Hour	Summary of Events and Information	Remarks and references to Appendices
Heytesbury	20/1/17	10 pm	Brigade left Southampton for France.	
Havre	22/1/17	10 pm	Left Havre 22/1/17 for Auxi-le-Chateau & billeted at OCCOCHES.	
Occoches	28/1/17	1. pm	Occupied Billets at NOEUX.	
Noeux	5/2/17	11 am	Occupied Billets at LUCHEUX.	
Lucheux	6/2/17	–	"D" Battery converted into a 6 gun Battery	

24/2/17

[illegible] Capt & Adjt.
for Lt Colonel
Comdg 29th Bde RAG.

290th Bde R.F.A.

Instructions regarding War Diaries and Intelligence Summaries are contained in F. S. Regs., Part II. and the Staff Manual respectively. Title pages will be prepared in manuscript.

WAR DIARY
or
INTELLIGENCE SUMMARY.
(Erase heading not required.)

Army Form C. 2118.

Place	Date	Hour	Summary of Events and Information	Remarks and references to Appendices
Heytesbury	20/1/17	10pm	Brigade left Southampton for France	
Havre	22/1/17	10pm	Left Havre 22/2/17 for Auxi-le-Chateau, & billeted at OCCOCHES.	
Occoches	28/2/17	11am	Occupied billets at NOEUX.	
Noeux	5/3/17	11am	Occupied billets at LUCHEUX	
Lucheux	27/2/17	12noon	"D" Battery converted into a 6 gun How Battery	

20/3/17.

[illegible] for Lt. Col.
Cdg 290th Bde R.F.A.

T2134. Wt. W708—776. 500000. 4/15. Sir J. C. & S.

290th Bde R.F.A.

Army Form C. 2118.

WAR DIARY
or
INTELLIGENCE SUMMARY.
(Erase heading not required.)

Instructions regarding War Diaries and Intelligence Summaries are contained in F. S. Regs., Part II. and the Staff Manual respectively. Title pages will be prepared in manuscript.

Place	Date	Hour	Summary of Events and Information	Remarks and references to Appendices
Lucheux	24/2/17	3pm	Brigade relieved the 245th Bde R.F.A. in the line & established Headquarters at LA-CAUCHIE. W H Kay capt by Lt & Adjt	
La Cauchie	17/3/17	4 pm	Received information that MONCHY had been vacated by the Enemy. W H Kay capt by Lt & Adjt	
La Cauchie	19/3/17		B/290th Bty ordered to advance & took up position at S. 11 D. 15 38.	51.B.S.W. W H Kay capt by Lt & Adjt
La Cauchie	20/3/17		Lt. Col. H. M. Clarke assumed command of B/290th Bty and C/291st Bty & established Headquarters at S. 14. C. 4. 5. W H Kay capt by Lt & Adjt	51.B.S.W.
La Cauchie	24/3/17	noon	A C & D Batteries 290th Bde R.F.A. not in action from 19-3-17. W H Kay capt by Lt & Adjt	
	27/3/17.		W H Kay capt by Lt & Adjt for Lt Col Cdg 290th Bde R.F.A.	

T2134. Wt. W708–776. 500000. 4/15. Sir J. C. & S.

Instructions regarding War Diaries and Intelligence Summaries are contained in F. S. Regs., Part II. and the Staff Manual respectively. Title pages will be prepared in manuscript.

WAR DIARY
or
INTELLIGENCE SUMMARY.
(Erase heading not required.)

Army Form C. 2118.

290 Bde R.F.A. 58 Div

Vol 4

Place	Date	Hour	Summary of Events and Information	Remarks and references to Appendices
La Cauchie	28/3/17		Hdqrs established at BOIRY-ST-RICTRUDE. C.H. Hagarty Lt + Adjt	
Boiry St Richard	31/3/17		A C + D Batteries went into action. C.H. Hagarty Lt + Adjt	
— " —	7/4/17		Group, under command of Col H.R. Clark, composed of A, B, C, D/290th + A/291st Btys, barraged whilst Infantry attacked HENIN-ST-COJEUL + CROISSELLES. C.H. Hagarty Lt + Adjt	
— " —	12/4/17		A B C + D Batteries came out of action. C.H. Hagarty Lt + Adjt	
— " —	13/4/17		Brigade proceeded to Bivouacs at B.26 A 0.9 + Hdqrs established at B.17 b. 3.6. C.H. Hagarty Capt + Adjt	
B.17 b 3.6	14/4/17		A B C + D Batteries in action at { A/290. C.7.c.8.3; B/290. C.7.c.7.9; C/290. C.1.c.3.1; D/290. B.12.b.3.2. C.H. Hagarty Capt + Adjt	
— " —	19/4/17		A + D Batteries out of action + proceeded to Wagon Lines at B.26 A 0.9. C.H. Hagarty Capt + Adjt	
— " —	22/4/17		B + C Batteries out of action + proceeded to Wagon Lines at B.26 A 0.9. C.H. Hagarty Capt + Adjt	
— " —	22/4/17		A + D Batteries in action at above positions. C.H. Hagarty Capt + Adjt for Lt Col Comdg 290th Bde R.F.A.	

T2134. Wt. W708-776. 500000. 4/15. Sir J. C. & S.

Vol 5

CONFIDENTIAL
****

W A R   D I A R Y

OF

290th Bde. R.F.A.

From 3/5/17

To 28/5/17

Instructions regarding War Diaries and Intelligence Summaries are contained in F. S. Regs., Part II. and the Staff Manual respectively. Title pages will be prepared in manuscript.

WAR DIARY
or
INTELLIGENCE SUMMARY.
(Erase heading not required.)

Army Form C. 2118.

Place	Date	Hour	Summary of Events and Information	Remarks and references to Appendices
B.17.B.3.6.	3/5/17.	3-30am	58th Divl Arty Group Barraged whilst Infantry delivered attack on BULLECOURT	
			[signature] Lt & Adjt.	
——"——	16/5/17.		58th Division in action night 15/16th May, 1917.	
			[signature] Lt & Adjt	
——"——	17/5/17		58th Divl. Arty Barraged whilst Infantry attacked & captured BULLECOURT. VILLAGE	
			[signature] Lt & Adjt.	

28/5/17

[signature] Lt & Adjt for Col
Comdg 290th Brigade R.F.A.

T2134. Wt. W708—776. 500000. 4/15. Sir J. C. & S.

Vol 6

Confidential

War Diary
of
290 Bde RFA

Army Form C. 2118.

Instructions regarding War Diaries and Intelligence Summaries are contained in F. S. Regs., Part II. and the Staff Manual respectively. Title pages will be prepared in manuscript.

WAR DIARY
or
INTELLIGENCE SUMMARY.
(Erase heading not required.)

Place	Date	Hour	Summary of Events and Information	Remarks and references to Appendices
B 12 d 15 85	night of 20/21 June.		Section of D/290 Bty advanced to C 22 d. 25 40 [signature] Lt + Adjt	
B 17 b 3 6	24/6/17	10.0am	290th Bde + 291st Bde R.F.A. formed Right Group Artillery, command taken over from Hdqrs 58th Divl Arty by Hdqrs 7th Divl Arty. [signature] Lt + Adjt	

Original

7

290th Brigade R.F.A.

WAR DIARY ~~or~~ INTELLIGENCE SUMMARY.

290 Bde RFA

Vol 7

Army Form C. 2118.

Instructions regarding War Diaries and Intelligence Summaries are contained in F. S. Regs., Part II. and the Staff Manual respectively. Title pages will be prepared in manuscript.

(Erase heading not required.)

Place	Date	Hour	Summary of Events and Information	Remarks and references to Appendices
B.17.b.5.6	June 28/29th		Commencement of the relief of the Brigade by 7th Divl Arty W H Lazenby Lt & Adjt	
	29th/30th		Completion of the relief by the 7th Divl Arty W H Lazenby Lt & Adjt	
	30/1st		Brigade moved to Wagon Lines at B.25.c.1.8 W H Lazenby Lt & Adjt	
	July 1/2nd		Brigade proceeded to Wagon Lines at P.33.c W H Lazenby Lt & Adjt	
	5th/6th		One section of each Battery relieved the 157th Brigade W H Lazenby Lt & Adjt	
	6th/7th		Remainder of the Batteries relieved the 157th Brigade W H Lazenby Lt & Adjt	
	9/7th		Headquarters of Brigade moved to Q.27.c.5.4 W H Lazenby Lt & Adjt	
	17th/18th		Brigade took over one section of each Battery being relieved by the 291st Brigade W H Lazenby Lt & Adjt	

T2134. Wt. W708–776. 500000. 4/15. Sir J. C. & S.

Instructions regarding War Diaries and Intelligence Summaries are contained in F. S. Regs., Part II. and the Staff Manual respectively. Title pages will be prepared in manuscript.

WAR DIARY
or
INTELLIGENCE SUMMARY.
(Erase heading not required.)

Army Form C. 2118.

Place	Date	Hour	Summary of Events and Information	Remarks and references to Appendices
	July 18th/19th		Relief of the Brigade by the 291st Brigade complete D H Hazenby Lt Adjt	
	do		Brigade Headquarters moved to Wagon Line at P.33.c D H Hazenby Lt Adjt	
	25th/26th		B & D Batteries went into action under the 211th Brigade D H Hazenby Lt Adjt	
			28/7/17 D H Hazenby Lt & Adjt for Lt Col Comdg 290th Brigade RFA	

T2134. Wt. W708-776. 500000. 4/15. Sir J. C. & S.

7

Instructions regarding War Diaries and Intelligence Summaries are contained in F. S. Regs., Part II. and the Staff Manual respectively. Title pages will be prepared in manuscript.

WAR DIARY
or
~~INTELLIGENCE SUMMARY.~~
(Erase heading not required.)

290 Bde R F A

Army Form C. 2118.

5 8

Vol 8

Place	Date	Hour	Summary of Events and Information	Remarks and references to Appendices
YTRES	2/8/17 5/8/17	}	Brigade moved to new position at HENINEL and relieved the 50th Bde RFA in action on 5/8/17. Brigade Hdqrs. at N.22.c.7.7, Wagon lines in M.17.a + b. W. G. Hazenby Capt + Adjt	
HENINEL	night of 20/8/17/21/8/17		Brigade relieved by 23rd A.F.A. Bde and proceeded to Wagon lines in M.17.a + b. W. G. Hazenby Capt + Adjt.	
BEAURAINS	night of 26/8/17/27/8/17		Brigade entrained at ARRAS and detrained 27/8/17 at GODEWAERSVELDE. W. G. Hazenby Capt + Adjt.	
	27/8/17		Wagon lines taken up at G.32.a. central. W. G. Hazenby Capt + Adjt.	
	30/8/17	2pm	Brigade moved to Wagon lines at H.25.d.5.3 vacated by 82 Bde R.F.A. W. G. Hazenby Capt + Adjt.	
	31/8/17		"A" "B" "C" + "D" Batteries commenced to relieve the 1st Australian Divl Arty in action. Battery positions in I.24.A. and I.17.c. W. G. Hazenby Capt + Adjt.	

T2134. Wt. W708—776. 500000. 4/15. Sir J. C. & S.

290th Brigade R.F.A.

Instructions regarding War Diaries and Intelligence Summaries are contained in F. S. Regs., Part II. and the Staff Manual respectively. Title pages will be prepared in manuscript.

WAR DIARY
or
~~INTELLIGENCE~~ SUMMARY.
(*Erase heading not required.*)

Army Form C. 2118.

Vol 9

Place	Date	Hour	Summary of Events and Information	Remarks and references to Appendices
	3-9-17		Brigade relieved by 110th Brigade R.F.A. and proceeded to Wagon Lines at HERZEELE.	
			[signature] Capt. & Adjt.	
HERZEELE	6-9-17		Brigade left Wagon Lines at HERZEELE and relieved 102 Brigade R.F.A. 1 Section per Battery in action 6/7th.	
	7-9-17		Rest of Brigade followed 7-9-17 and relief of 102 Brigade completed by noon 7-9-17.	
			Wagon Lines at H.1.b. and B.25.d.	
			Headquarters at I.1.d.	
			[signature] Capt. & Adjt.	
I.1.a	14-9-17		Headquarters moved to WILSONS FARM. Command of Right Group, 58th Divisional Artillery - consisting of 290th Brigade R.F.A. and 155 A.F.A. Brigade - taken over relieving 155th A.F.A. Brigade.	
			[signature] Capt. & Adjt.	

T2134. Wt. W708-776. 500000. 4/15. Sir J. C. & S.

Instructions regarding War Diaries and Intelligence Summaries are contained in F. S. Regs., Part II. and the Staff Manual respectively. Title pages will be prepared in manuscript.

290th Brigade RFA

WAR DIARY
or
~~INTELLIGENCE SUMMARY.~~
(Erase heading not required.)

Army Form C. 2118.

Place	Date	Hour	Summary of Events and Information	Remarks and references to Appendices
WILSONS FARM.	19th/20th		Barrage and attack by 58th Division. C H [illegible] Capt & Adjt	
"	25th/26th		Barrage and attack by 58th Division C H [illegible] Capt & Adjt	
"	27th/28th		84th A.F.A. Brigade relieved 155th A.F.A Brigade in the Right Group. C H [illegible] Capt & Adjt	
"	30/7		Right Group Command taken over by 84th A F A Brigade 290th Brigade Headquarters moved to I.1.d. C H [illegible] Capt & Adjt.	

T2134. Wt. W708—776. 500000. 4/15. Sir J. C. & S.

4 58

290th Brigade R.F.A.

Instructions regarding War Diaries and Intelligence Summaries are contained in F. S. Regs., Part II. and the Staff Manual respectively. Title pages will be prepared in manuscript.

WAR DIARY
or
~~INTELLIGENCE SUMMARY.~~
(Erase heading not required.)

Army Form C. 2118.

Appx Vol 10
Oct 17

Place	Date	Hour	Summary of Events and Information	Remarks and references to Appendices
	17/10/17		Brigade Headquarters moved to CHEDDAR VILLA. C.17.C.75.00. [illegible] Capt & Adjt	
	18/10/17		Command of No. 3 Group (290th and 291st Brigades R.F.A), 9th Divisional Artillery taken over. [illegible] Capt & Adjt	
	23/10/17		Wagon Lines moved from B.25.d. to C.25.C. CANAL BANK. [illegible] Capt & Adjt	
			Operations in the YPRES Battle were carried out on 4th, 12th, 21st, 25th, and 30th October. [illegible] Capt & Adjt	

T2134. Wt. W708—776. 500000. 4/15. Sir J. C. & S.

13

290th Brigade RFA

Instructions regarding War Diaries and Intelligence Summaries are contained in F. S. Regs., Part II. and the Staff Manual respectively. Title pages will be prepared in manuscript.

WAR DIARY
or
~~INTELLIGENCE SUMMARY.~~
(Erase heading not required.)

Army Form C. 2118. 58

Vol 11

Place	Date	Hour	Summary of Events and Information	Remarks and references to Appendices
	1917			
CHEDDAR VILLA	31/10/17		Brigade Headquarters moved to Wagon Lines at Canal Bank on being relieved by 1st Divl Arty. William S Hagarty Capt & Adjt	
	9/10th Nov.		Brigade proceeded to Billets at Polincove spending the night at WORMHOUDT. William S Hagarty Capt & Adjt	
	12/13th Nov.		Brigade proceeded to Billets in the ESTREE AREA spending the night at DESVRES. Brigade Headquarters established at MONTCAVREL. William S Hagarty Capt & Adjt 290th Brigade RFA.	

T2134. Wt. W708—776. 500000. 4/15. Sir J. C. & S.

4

D.A.G.
3rd Echelon. Base

Herewith War Diary of this Brigade for December 1917.

In the Field
31-12-17

[illegible] Capt. & Adjt.
for Lt. Col.
Comdg 290 Bde R.F.A.

290 Brigade R.F.A. 58

Instructions regarding War Diaries and Intelligence Summaries are contained in F. S. Regs., Part II. and the Staff Manual respectively. Title pages will be prepared in manuscript.

WAR DIARY
or
~~INTELLIGENCE~~ SUMMARY.
(Erase heading not required.)

Army Form C. 2118.

Vol 12

Place	Date	Hour	Summary of Events and Information	Remarks and references to Appendices
ESTREE AREA.	4/12/17		Brigade proceeded from ESTREE Area by road and occupied billets at MERCK St LIEVIN for the night. [illegible] Capt & Adjt.	
	5/12/17		Brigade continued its march to forward area billeting for the night at BROXEELE. [illegible] Capt & Adjt.	
	6/12/17		March continued and billets occupied for the night at ZERMEZEELE. [illegible] Capt & Adjt.	
	7/12/17		Brigade continued march and occupied Wagon Lines at ELVERDINGHE. [illegible] Capt & Adjt.	
	9/12/17		One Section of each Battery of the Brigade relieved the 82nd and 83rd Brigades in action. [illegible] Capt & Adjt.	

Army Form C. 2118.

290 Brigade R+A

WAR DIARY

or

~~INTELLIGENCE~~ SUMMARY.

(Erase heading not required.)

Instructions regarding War Diaries and Intelligence Summaries are contained in F. S. Regs., Part II. and the Staff Manual respectively. Title pages will be prepared in manuscript.

Place	Date	Hour	Summary of Events and Information	Remarks and references to Appendices
	10/2/17		Relief of 82nd and 83rd Brigades completed.	
			Batte Headquarters established at CANE POST (C. 9. a. 5. 5)	
			Ref map St JULIEN 28 N.W. 2 1/10,000.	
			[illegible] Capt + Adjt	
	17/2/17		Brigade Wagon Lines moved to C 26 C. (Ref. St JULIEN 28 NW.2 1/10000)	
			[illegible] Capt + Adjt.	
			290 Brigade R + A.	

T2134. Wt. W708—776. 500000. 4/15. Sir J. C. & S.

9

Instructions regarding War Diaries and Intelligence Summaries are contained in F. S. Regs., Part II. and the Staff Manual respectively. Title pages will be prepared in manuscript.

290th Brigade R.F.A.

WAR DIARY
or
~~INTELLIGENCE SUMMARY.~~
(Erase heading not required.)

Army Form C. 2118.

Vol 13

Place	Date	Hour	Summary of Events and Information	Remarks and references to Appendices
CANE POST.	Jany	12th/13th	Brigade relieved in action by 157th Brigade R.F.A.	
			Lt-Colonel D.S.O.	
		13/14th	One Section per Battery on night of 12/13th relieved, the remaining sections on night of 13th/14th. Command passing to the 157th Brigade on the morning of the 14th, when the Brigade moved to Wagon Lines in HAMHOEK AREA.	
			Lt-Colonel D.S.O.	
		15th	Lt. Colonel A. N. Clark D.S.O. relinquished command of Brigade	
			Lt-Colonel D.S.O.	
		16th	Lt Colonel W.A.F. Jones D.S.O. assumed Command of Brigade.	
			Lt. Colonel D.S.O.	
		22nd	Brigade entrained at PROVEN to proceed to 5th Army Area.	
			Lt. Colonel D.S.O.	
		23rd	Brigade detrained at VILLERS BRETONNEUX and proceeded to Billets in HANGARD.	
			Lt. Colonel D.S.O.	

T2134. Wt. W708–776. 500000. 4/15. Sir J. C. & S.

Instructions regarding War Diaries and Intelligence Summaries are contained in F. S. Regs., Part II. and the Staff Manual respectively. Title pages will be prepared in manuscript.

290th Brigade RFA

WAR DIARY
or
INTELLIGENCE SUMMARY.
(Erase heading not required.)

Army Form C. 2118.

Place	Date	Hour	Summary of Events and Information	Remarks and references to Appendices
	Jany 28th		Brigade marched from HANBARD to the forward area spending the night at GRUNY. Lt Colonel DSO	
	" 29th		Brigade continued the march to forward area and occupied billets in BABOEUF. Lt Colonel DSO	
	" 30th		Brigade Headquarters transferred to LIEZ. "A", "B" and "C" Batteries relieved the 221st Regiment of French Artillery in the line. Lt Colonel DSO	
	31st		Lt Colonel W.A.F. Jones DSO. took over Command of Group of Artillery consisting of A/290, B/290, C/290, and "O" and "Z" Batteries of the 5th Army Brigade R.H.A. Lt Colonel DSO W.A.F. Jones Comdg 290 Brigade RFA	

Instructions regarding War Diaries and Intelligence Summaries are contained in F. S. Regs., Part II. and the Staff Manual respectively. Title pages will be prepared in manuscript.

WAR DIARY
or
~~INTELLIGENCE SUMMARY.~~
(Erase heading not required.)

Army Form C. 2118.

290 Bde RFA

Vol 14

Place	Date	Hour	Summary of Events and Information	Remarks and references to Appendices
	Feb 16.		General Bell, United States Army, inspected some of the Battery positions.	
	Feb 17.		Working party, consisting of 3 officers and 110 men of the 82nd Brigade RFA (18th Divn) reported for work on rear positions.	
	Feb 21		Captain R.M. Hinman, RFA, was posted to Command B/290, vice Captain (A/Major) J. F. MacDonell, temporarily transferred to D.A.C. pending further posting.	
	Feb 22		Major F. L. Congreve M.C. R.F.A reported for a month's attachment to B.H.Q.	
	Feb. 24		5th Army Brigade RHA, (QUESSY Sector) and 290th Brigade RFA (VENDEUIL Sector) Completed first half of mutual relief.	
	Feb 25		Second half of relief completed, 290th Brigade taking over defence of QUESSY Sector from 6 p.m., Brigade Headquarters at QUESSY, covering the 175th Infantry Brigade.	
	Feb. 26		Captain F.C. Moore, RFA posted to Command of C/290. vice Lieut (A/Major) W. H. Bevan	
	Feb. 27		Lieut (A/Major) W. H Bevan wounded and evacuated.	
	Feb. 28		In consequence of German activity on the French front C/290 ordered to position south of the river to reinforce 291st Bde. This order was cancelled later, but Wagon Lines of Brigade stood by harnessed up until midnight. Quiet night.	

28.2.18.

W. H. [illegible] Lt. Colonel
Cmdg 290th Brigade RFA.

T2134. Wt. W708—776. 500000. 4/15. Sir J. C. & S.

14 1

Instructions regarding War Diaries and Intelligence Summaries are contained in F. S. Regs., Part II. and the Staff Manual respectively. Title pages will be prepared in manuscript.

WAR DIARY or ~~INTELLIGENCE SUMMARY.~~ MARCH, 1918

290 Bde. R.F.A.

(Erase heading not required.)

Army Form C. 2118.

58 Divn

Place	Date	Hour	Summary of Events and Information 290 Brigade R.F.A.	Remarks and references to Appendices
In the Field.	MARCH 1918.		Vol 15	
	1 to 20.		All batteries of Brigade engaged in constructing and improving positions for defence of Battle Zone. Harassing fire nightly on ST. FIRMIN & LA FÈRE. Lt.Col. WAF JONES DSO proceeded to England on 14 days' course on 13th. – Major F.L. CONGREVE MC assumed command of the Brigade. Lt. G. RUSSELL proceeded on 14 days leave to England on 17th. 2Lt H.A. HATFIELD became A/Adjt.	
	21	3.45 – 4.5 AM	"Counter Preparation" carried out by all Batteries.	
		4.30 AM	Enemy bombardment began. Brigade again opened on "Counter Preparation"	
		9.10 AM ~~4.30 AM~~	Enemy reported in Brickfields on West side of OISE & SAMBRE CANAL opposite ST. FIRMIN Gate. Concentration of all batteries ordered on West bank of canal. Communication with batteries now only by orderlies.	
		9.30 AM.	A/290 Forward Gun destroyed & detachment withdrawn after firing about 200 rds. Situation obscure owing to dense mist. Nothing heard of B/290's Forward Section all day	
		11.15 AM.	Enemy massing behind FERME ROUGE (E. of road QUESSY – F[ORT] LIEZ) – batteries directed to fire on them.	
		11.15 – 7.30 pm	Enemy three times repulsed by artillery attempting to debouch from FERME ROUGE	

2.

Instructions regarding War Diaries and Intelligence Summaries are contained in F. S. Regs., Part II. and the Staff Manual respectively. Title pages will be prepared in manuscript.

WAR DIARY ~~or~~ ~~INTELLIGENCE SUMMARY.~~ MARCH, 1918 (cont.)

(Erase heading not required.)

290 Brigade R.F.A.

Army Form C. 2118.

Place	Date	Hour	Summary of Events and Information	Remarks and references to Appendices
MARCH (cont)				
	21	1pm	O/R.H.A. reported for duty. Put into action at VOUVEL-TERGNIER Cross roads.	
		4pm	Enemy in DISTILLERY at FARGNIERS.	
		8.15pm	After dusk enemy succeeded in capturing B/290's 4-gun position & FORT LIEZ B/290 gun destroyed by 106 H.E. In consequence of capture of FORT LIEZ in their rear 4 guns C/290 destroyed & detachments withdrawn. A/290 & D/290 ordered to withdraw	
		11.30pm	Enemy holding line of CROZAT canal at QUESSY. 290 B.H.Q. moved to VIRY-NOUREUIL.	
		M'D'NT.	Batteries in action in BOIS HALLOT - A/290 5 guns, C/290 2 guns (withdrawn from CONDREN) O/R.H.A. 6 guns, D/290 4 hows. It was impossible to withdraw forward section of D/290 owing to roads being destroyed ~~by~~ by shell fire. The 2 hows were therefore blown up.	
			CASUALTIES. 2[Lt] C.M. Hicks & 2Lt. H. WN. FANE (B/290) missing, believed captured, 15 O.R. missing; Killed 4 OR; wounded ~~[illegible]~~ 2LT. F.D. KEANE + 10 O.R. - Horses 12 killed; 4 wounded	
	22	6.30AM.	Batteries opened on TERGNIER & fired on targets ordered by B.H.Q. or F.O.O.'s After dusk batteries moved to ROUEZ area - B.H.Q. moved to CHAUNY.	
	23.	3AM.	Rolling barrage commenced with object of driving enemy back over CROZAT canal.	

T2134. Wt. W708—776. 500000. 4/15. Sir J. C. & S.

3.

Instructions regarding War Diaries and Intelligence Summaries are contained in F. S. Regs., Part II. and the Staff Manual respectively. Title pages will be prepared in manuscript.

WAR DIARY MARCH, 1918
or
~~INTELLIGENCE SUMMARY.~~
(Erase heading not required.)

290 Brigade R.F.A.

Army Form C. 2118.

Place	Date	Hour	Summary of Events and Information	Remarks and references to Appendices
March (cont.)				
	23 cont.	10.30	French Infantry retired on FRIÈRES WOOD.	
		11.30 AM.	12 inch How. on Railway mounting attached to Group - given BUTTE as target - retired 4.30 pm.	
		12.30 pm.	O/RHA. detached from Group.	
		1.10 pm.	Batteries (A/290 5 guns, C/290 2 guns, D/290 4 hows.) ordered to retire on VILLEQUIER-AUMONT + RUE de CAUMONT. Positions taken up by A/C/D/290 between CAUMONT + RUE de CAUMONT. Objectives East of road VIRY-NOUREUIL - NOUREUIL.	
	24th	2 AM.	B.H.Q. moved to ABBÉCOURT	
		9 AM.	B.H.Q. moved to QUIERZY	
		6 AM.	2 - 18 prs. C/290 out of action (buffer trouble). Group now = A/290 5 guns, D/290 4 - 4.5 hows. A/290 + D/290 withdrew to positions near BETHANCOURT-en-VAUX. Enemy reported in CAUMONT necessitated further withdrawal to positions between CRÉPIGNY + MONDESCOURT. Objectives BÉTHANCOURT + NEUFLIEUX. Further advance of enemy caused withdrawal of both batteries to BABŒUF.	
	25th	NOON	H.Q. moved to RUE MILLON	
			Acting on orders from C.R.A. 18th D.A. batteries moved South of River OISE during night of 24/25 March. A/290 + D/290 took up positions 1000x S.E. of VARESNES. These	

T2134. Wt. W708–776. 500000. 4/15. Sir J. C. & S.

4.

Instructions regarding War Diaries and Intelligence Summaries are contained in F. S. Regs., Part II. and the Staff Manual respectively. Title pages will be prepared in manuscript.

WAR DIARY MARCH, 1918
or
~~INTELLIGENCE~~ SUMMARY. 290 Brigade R.F.A.

(Erase heading not required.)

Army Form C. 2118.

Place	Date	Hour	Summary of Events and Information	Remarks and references to Appendices
March (cont)				
	25 (cont)		positions becoming untenable A/290 moved during night to RUE MILLON and	
	26th	10AM.	in morning (26th) to CUTS. Thence A + D/290 moved to positions in BOIS de MANICAMP where they remained until 58th D.A. was moved from area on April 2nd	
			HQ. moved from RUE MILLON to BESMÉ.	
		M'D'N'T.	2 sections each of 407, 408 R.F.A., 3.18 prs. A/291, 2.18 prs. B/291, 1-18 pr. C/291 + 4.4.5 Hows D/291 came into action in area BOIS de FÈVÈ under orders of O.C. 290 Bde.	
	27th	NIGHT	Most of these guns were ~~withdrawn~~ removed to East side of OISE + AISNE canal leaving 1-18 pr. A/291 + 2-hows D/291 under command of O.C. 290 Bde. These guns remained until group came out of action on April 2.	
			Harassing fire was carried out by day and (chiefly) by night on enemy's communications CHAUNY-MAREST-DAMPCOURT.	
	28		B/290 - reconstituted as 4 gun battery came into action at BAC d'ARBLINCOURT under orders of O.C. 291 Bde. R.F.A. The guns (one section each of 407, 408 R.F.A.) were taken over in action.	
	29 30 31		Usual harassing fire on enemy's Lines of Communication in Brigade Zone.	

W. M. Jones Lt. Col.
Cg 290th Bde R.F.A.

T2134. Wt. W708—776. 500000. 4/15. Sir J. C. & S.

58th Div.

WAR DIARY

Headquarters,

290th BRIGADE, R.F.A.

A P R I L

1 9 1 8

11 58

Instructions regarding War Diaries and Intelligence Summaries are contained in F. S. Regs., Part II. and the Staff Manual respectively. Title pages will be prepared in manuscript.

WAR DIARY or INTELLIGENCE SUMMARY.

290 Brigade R.F.A

(Erase heading not required.)

Army Form C. 2118.

98 16

Place	Date	Hour	Summary of Events and Information	Remarks and references to Appendices
	1/4/18.		Headquarters BESMÉ, Batteries in action FÈVE WOOD, "C" Battery brought two guns into action, having been out of action for a week.	
	2/4/18.		Headquarters and Batteries moved to BERLANCOURT in the evening, the French Batteries covering the front we vacated.	
	3/4/18.		The Brigade marched to VILLERS-COTTERETS and LONG PONT, "A" and "C" Batteries to the former place H.Q., "B" and "D" Batteries to the latter, starting at 8 pm.	
	4/4/18.		Entrained for AMIENS.	
	5/4/18.		Brigade detrained at LONGEAU between 2 am and 12 noon and camped on the BOULEVARDS, AMIENS.	
	6/4/18.		OC Brigade and Battery Commanders proceeded to inspect battery positions near FOUILLOY, "A" Battery and 1 Section each of B. C. and D. Batteries went into action after dark, relieving Batteries of the 177th Brigade, the Brigade now coming under orders of 5 Australian Division R.A.	
	7/4/18.		Relief completed, remaining sections of "B" "C" and "D" going into action after dark.	

T2134. Wt. W708-776. 500000. 4/15. Sir J. C. & S.

Page II.

Army Form C. 2118.

Instructions regarding War Diaries and Intelligence Summaries are contained in F. S. Regs., Part II. and the Staff Manual respectively. Title pages will be prepared in manuscript.

WAR DIARY

~~INTELLIGENCE~~ SUMMARY.

290 Brigade R.F.A.

(Erase heading not required.)

Place	Date	Hour	Summary of Events and Information	Remarks and references to Appendices
	9/4/18		Battery positions heavily shelled from 4 a.m. to 7 a.m., front system also shelled with gas shell, 2/Lieut. L.L. Hart gassed at Brigade O.P. and admitted to Hospital. A large number of officers who had been detained at the Base since the beginning of the push rejoined the Brigade.	
	10/4/18		One gun of A Battery brought into action in a forward position as an anti-tank gun.	
	11-17/4/18		Very little hostile activity.	
	18/4/18		Commenced mutual relief with the 298th Army Brigade in the VILLERS-BRETONNEUX Sector.	
	19/4/18		Relief completed, guns handed over in situ, the Brigade coming under orders of 58th D.A. covering front held by the 8th Divl Infantry.	
	23/4/18		Lt. Colonel JONES D.S.O. took command of the Group composed of 96th 169th and 290th Brigades, having Headquarters at 173 Infantry Brigade Headquarters.	

Page 3

Instructions regarding War Diaries and Intelligence Summaries are contained in F. S. Regs., Part II. and the Staff Manual respectively. Title pages will be prepared in manuscript.

WAR DIARY

290th Brigade R.F.A.

~~INTELLIGENCE~~ SUMMARY.

(Erase heading not required.)

Army Form C. 2118.

Place	Date	Hour	Summary of Events and Information	Remarks and references to Appendices
	24/4/18.		German attack on our Sector commencing with a very heavy bombardment at 4 am. Between 12 noon and 2 pm Batteries were withdrawn to rear positions, leaving 5 Hows and 1-18 pdr. At 10 pm a counter attack was made, the enemy being driven back to his starting point, and at some points farther, the 5 Hows. and 1-18 pdr being recovered. During the day Majors Henman and Moore and 2nd Lts Meathrel, Morice and Pearson were wounded and admitted to Hospital. 2/Lt WRIGHT who went forward during the morning was wounded and captured. Casualties 6 Officers and 64 O.Rs.	
	25/4/18.		Mutual relief carried out with 82nd Brigade in the afternoon, the 290 Brigade going to reserve positions in T. 3.	
	28/4/18.		Colonel W.A.F. JONES DSO rejoined and took command of the Brigade on JONES' GROUP ceasing to exist. At 8.30 pm. Headquarters and all Batteries were withdrawn to Wagon Lines near CAGNY.	
	29-30-4-18.		Brigade proceeded by route march to rest area in EPAGNE and EPAGNETTE, halting the night at	

Page 4

Instructions regarding War Diaries and Intelligence Summaries are contained in F. S. Regs., Part II. and the Staff Manual respectively. Title pages will be prepared in manuscript.

WAR DIARY
or
INTELLIGENCE SUMMARY.
(Erase heading not required.)

Army Form C. 2118.

Place	Date	Hour	Summary of Events and Information	Remarks and references to Appendices
	29-30-4-16		CROUY. Brigade Headquarters established at CHATEAU EPAGNE during the afternoon of the 30th. Total casualties for the month. 7 Officers and 75 other ranks.	

W. A. Jones.
Lt-Colonel DSO
Commanding
290 Brigade RFA

T2134. Wt. W708—776. 500000. 4/15. Sir J. C. & S.

10

290 Brigade R.F.A.

WAR DIARY
or
~~INTELLIGENCE~~ SUMMARY.
(Erase heading not required.)

Army Form C. 2118.

Instructions regarding War Diaries and Intelligence Summaries are contained in F. S. Regs., Part II. and the Staff Manual respectively. Title pages will be prepared in manuscript.

1917

Place	Date	Hour	Summary of Events and Information	Remarks and references to Appendices
	May 1-16th		Brigade remained at Rest in EPAGNE and EPAGNETTE.	
	3rd		T. Lt. A/Major W. Taylor M.C. posted to Brigade to Command B/290	
	11th		"B" Battery proceeded by road to SAILLY-LE-SEC to act as depot Battery at the Reserve Army Artillery School.	
	13th		Major General C.E.D. Budworth C.B., C.M.G., M.V.O. R.A., G.O.C., R.A. Fourth Army, inspected Gun Parks, Horse lines and horses in the morning and attended the 58th Divisional Artillery Horse Show in the afternoon.	
	16th		Brigade, less B/290, proceeded by route march and spent the night at BOURDON.	
	17		Brigade continued the route march and occupied the Wagon Lines of the 169th Brigade R.F.A. in the neighbourhood of BAVELINCOURT, one section of each Battery relieving ~~the~~ 169th Brigade R.F.A. in the line.	

D. D. & L., London, E.C. (A8004) Wt W1771/M2031 750,000 5/17 Sch. 52 Forms/C2118/14

II

290 Brigade RFA

WAR DIARY
or
~~INTELLIGENCE~~ SUMMARY.
(Erase heading not required.)

Army Form C. 2118.

Instructions regarding War Diaries and Intelligence Summaries are contained in F. S. Regs., Part II. and the Staff Manual respectively. Title pages will be prepared in manuscript.

Place	Date	Hour	Summary of Events and Information	Remarks and references to Appendices
	May 18th		Remaining two sections of each Battery relieved the 169th Brigade RFA. Brigade Headquarters moved to HENENCOURT CHATEAU. Lt Colonel N.A.F. JONES. DSO. taking over the defence of the line, covering, with the following Batteries, A/290, C/290, D/290 and 407th Battery, 1500 yards of the front due W. of ALBERT.	
	22nd		Major General J. VAUGHAN, Inspector General of Horse Management, inspected all horses of the Brigade in the Wagon Lines.	
	23rd		The following Awards were made:-	
			Mentioned in Despatches.	
			2/Lieut L. F. Robinson.	
			Military Medal.	
			925611. Driver Clarkson. R.	
			950 62 Gunner. Umphray P.	
			926161 Driver. Bridle H.	
			925793. Driver. Castle. W.	
			690402 L/Bdr. Hodgkinson. P.	
			94409. Gunner. Martin A	
			925619. Gunner. Templeman. G W.	

D. D. & L., London, E.C.
(A8004) Wt W1771/M2031 750,000 5/17 Sch. 52 Forms/C2118/14

Sheet III

Instructions regarding War Diaries and Intelligence Summaries are contained in F. S. Regs., Part II. and the Staff Manual respectively. Title pages will be prepared in manuscript.

290 Brigade R.F.A.

WAR DIARY

or

~~INTELLIGENCE~~ ~~SUMMARY.~~

(Erase heading not required.)

Army Form C. 2118.

Place	Date	Hour	Summary of Events and Information	Remarks and references to Appendices
	May 23.		Awards (contd)	
			Bar to the Military Medal.	
			30796 A/L/Bdr. T. Hutchings M.M.	
	24th/25th		407th Battery relieved by A/236.	
	28th/29th		A/236 Battery relieved by A/83.	

W.A. Jones

Lt Colonel D.S.O.
Commanding
290 Brigade R.F.A.

D. D. & L., London, E.C.
(A8004) Wt W1771/M2031 750,000 5/17 Sch. 52 Forms/C2118/14

Instructions regarding War Diaries and Intelligence Summaries are contained in F. S. Regs., Part II. and the Staff Manual respectively. Title pages will be prepared in manuscript.

WAR DIARY or ~~INTELLIGENCE SUMMARY.~~

290 Brigade R.F.A.

(Erase heading not required.)

Army Form C. 2118.

Vol 18

Place	Date	Hour	Summary of Events and Information	Remarks and references to Appendices
1918	June 1st		2/Lieut. L.F. BECKH joined the Brigade and was posted to A/290.	
	2nd		Headquarters 18th Divisional Artillery relieved Headquarters of the 58th Divisional Artillery in the line.	
			The 55th Infantry Brigade 18th Division took over the front covered by the Brigade.	
			2/Lieut. R.C. Cook M.C. transferred to 58 Divisional Trench Mortars.	
	3rd		2/Lieut. W.T. KING joined the Brigade and was posted to C/290.	
			Brig. General C.M. ROSS-JOHNSON C.B. C.M.G. D.S.O. G.O.C.R.A. III Corps visited all Battery positions.	
	6th		Advance parties of Headquarters and all Batteries of the 169th Army Brigade R.F.A. came up to see the front and Battery positions. O.C. 169th Brigade spending the night at Brigade Headquarters.	
			2/Lieut. J.L. HADFIELD and 2/Lieut. P.F. MUMFORD joined the Brigade and were posted to B/290 and A/290 respectively.	

T2134. Wt. W708—776. 500000. 4/15. Sir J. C. & S.

Sheet II

Instructions regarding War Diaries and Intelligence Summaries are contained in F. S. Regs., Part II. and the Staff Manual respectively. Title pages will be prepared in manuscript.

WAR DIARY
or
~~INTELLIGENCE SUMMARY.~~
(*Erase heading not required.*)

Army Form C. 2118.

Place	Date	Hour	Summary of Events and Information	Remarks and references to Appendices
	1918			
June	7th		169th Army Brigade R.F.A relieved the Brigade in action. Headquarters and Batteries moved to their Wagon Lines at BAVELINCOURT.	
	9th		Brigade proceeded by route march and occupied billets at ARGOEUVES 4 miles WEST of AMIENS. On arrival in this area the 58th Division came under the XXIInd Corps.	
	10th		"B" Battery returned from the School at SAILLY-LE-SEC and rejoined the Brigade.	
	10th–18th		Batteries and Battery Staffs trained in mounted work with a view to quicken up drill and movement. A certain number of officers sent out almost daily to reconnoitre the neighbouring fronts of the Australian Corps and 31st French Corps, NORTH and SOUTH of AMIENS respectively in case the Division was required for reinforcing either of these fronts.	
	16th		Captain C.F.H. PHILLIPS joined the Brigade and was posted 2nd in command of D/290.	

T2134. Wt. W708—776. 506000. 4/15. Sir J. C. & S.

Sheet III

Instructions regarding War Diaries and Intelligence Summaries are contained in F. S. Regs., Part II. and the Staff Manual respectively. Title pages will be prepared in manuscript.

WAR DIARY
or
INTELLIGENCE SUMMARY.
(Erase heading not required.)

Army Form C. 2118.

Place	Date	Hour	Summary of Events and Information	Remarks and references to Appendices
June	1918 19th		Brigade proceeded by route march and occupied Wagon Lines at BAVELINCOURT, returning to the III Corps.	
	20th		Brigade relieved the 236th Brigade 47th Division in the line. Headquarters being established in the Quarry at D.4.c.2.4. Lt Colonel W.A.F. JONES D.S.O. taking over the defence of the line with the 4 Batteries of the Brigade and the 377th Battery 169th Army Brigade R.F.A. Covering the front held by the 173rd Infantry Brigade astride the ALBERT – AMIENS Road. The daily allotment of ammunition being 1000 rounds 18-pdrs and 200 rounds 4.5 Hows, for the Group.	
	23rd		Major General F.W. RAMSAY C.M.G. D.S.O. G.O.C. 58 Division inspected Battery positions accompanied by the C.R.A. Position of 377th Battery shelled by 5.9 Battery 6 rounds falling in the Battery position, wounding 1 officer and disabling 1 gun.	
	24		4.2 Battery consistently shelled vicinity of	

T2134. Wt. W708—776. 500000. 4/15. Sir J. C. & S.

Sheet IV

Instructions regarding War Diaries and Intelligence Summaries are contained in F. S. Regs., Part II. and the Staff Manual respectively. Title pages will be prepared in manuscript.

WAR DIARY
or
INTELLIGENCE SUMMARY.
(Erase heading not required.)

Army Form C. 2118.

Place	Date	Hour	Summary of Events and Information	Remarks and references to Appendices
	1918			
June	24.		A/290 and B/290 positions, firing about 300 Rounds, 1 gun of B/290 receiving one or more direct hits, the gun being destroyed and 1 O.R wounded.	
	27th		Lieut J. RADFORD-NORCOP joined the Divisional Artillery as Horse Adviser 58th Divisional Artillery and was attached to this Brigade.	
			W. D. V. Jones Lt: Col: D.S.O:, Comdg: 290th Brigade, R.F.A.	
June	1st		The following awards were made:-	
			MILITARY CROSS	
			2/Lieut T. DUNN	
			Lieut (A/Major) F C MOORE	
			DISTINGUISHED CONDUCT MEDAL	
	"		925409 Sergeant STEELE. E.E.	
"	2nd		926310 B.S.M. GOOD S.H.	
			W. D. V. Jones Lt: Col: D.S.O:, Comdg: 290th Brigade, R.F.A.	

T2134. Wt. W708—776. 500000. 4/15. Sir J. C. & S.

Instructions regarding War Diaries and Intelligence Summaries are contained in F. S. Regs., Part II. and the Staff Manual respectively. Title pages will be prepared in manuscript.

WAR DIARY
290 Brigade R.F.A.
~~INTELLIGENCE~~ SUMMARY.
(*Erase heading not required.*)

Army Form C. 2118.

VR 19

Place	Date	Hour	Summary of Events and Information	Remarks and references to Appendices
	July 1st		On the night of June 30th/July 1st all batteries of the Group fired a barrage in connection with an operation by the 12th and 18th Divisions on our Left.	
	" 4th		In the early morning of the 4th all Batteries of the Group fired a barrage in conjunction with an attack by the Australian Corps on our right.	
	" 8th		At 9 pm received the order Battle Stations Practice	
	" 10th		377th Battery was relieved by B/108 Battery R.F.A.	
	" 12th		Lt Colonel W.A.F. JONES D.S.O. proceeded on 14 days leave to England. Major J.C. BECKHAM M.C assumed command of the Group	
	" 18th		2/Lieut F.G. THOMPSON was transferred to 58th Division Trench Mortars.	
	" 20th		2/Lieut A.A. HARRIS joined the Brigade and was posted to "C" Battery	
	" 25th		All Batteries of the Group fired a barrage from 10 am. to 12 noon while a daylight raid was carried out by the Infantry.	
	" 26th		58th Divisional Zone was moved slightly to the Right,	

T2134. Wt. W708—776. 500000. 4/15. Sir J. C. & S.

Instructions regarding War Diaries and Intelligence Summaries are contained in F. S. Regs., Part II. and the Staff Manual respectively. Title pages will be prepared in manuscript.

WAR DIARY
or
INTELLIGENCE SUMMARY.
(Erase heading not required.)

Army Form C. 2118.

Place	Date	Hour	Summary of Events and Information	Remarks and references to Appendices
	July	26th	being reconstructed into two Groups. Right Group consisting of 5th Army Brigade R.H.A. B/86 Bde R.F.A and D/86th Bde R.F.A., Left Group consisting of the 291st Brigade R.F.A and this Brigade as a sub-Group. All Batteries remained in their present position, Brigade Headquarters moving to D.9.d.78.52.	
	"	29th	Lieut. C.W.D. Jones was transferred to XXII Corps R.A.	
			The allotment of ammunition throughout the month for harassing fire was 400 rounds for 18-pdrs and 75 rounds for 4.5" Howitzers for Group	

J.E. Beckham [signature]
Major M.C.
for Lt. Colonel
Commanding 290 Brigade R.F.A.

T2134. Wt. W708—776. 506000. 4/15. Sir J. C. & S.

58th Divl . Artillery

290th BRIGADE, R. F. A.

A U G U S T   1 9 1 8.

11

Instructions regarding War Diaries and Intelligence Summaries are contained in F. S. Regs., Part II. and the Staff Manual respectively. Title pages will be prepared in manuscript.

WAR DIARY or ~~INTELLIGENCE~~ SUMMARY.

290 Brigade R.F.A.

(Erase heading not required.)

Army Form C. 2118.

Vol 20

Place	Date	Hour	Summary of Events and Information	Remarks and references to Appendices
	July 31st		Lt Colonel W.A.F. Jones DSO returned from 14 days leave to England.	
			During the night of 31st July/1st August and 1st/2nd August the Brigade was relieved in the line by the 25th Divisional Artillery. The Brigade proceeded to Wagon Lines at BAVELINCOURT.	
August	2nd		Brigade and Battery Commanders proceeded by lorry to reconnoitre positions in the neighbourhood of WELLCOME WOOD.	
			Capt C.A. Phillips was wounded and struck off strength.	
"	3rd		Reconnaissance continued and in the evening Batteries commenced to dump ammunition at the Battery positions. at 600 Rds per gun.	
"	4th		Capt G.R. Johnston joined the Brigade and was posted as 2nd in Command of D/290.	
"	6		Owing to an enemy raid penetrating to the positions selected, fresh positions had to be selected for C/290 and D/290.	
"	7th		Brigade Headquarters moved to Battle Headquarters at J.22.d.2.4 with 174th Infy Bde. All the Batteries coming into action in the evening.	
	8th		Barrage fired at 4.20 am in conjunction with an Infantry attack. All Batteries advanced to forward positions in the evening, Headquarters being	

T2134. Wt. W708—776. 500000. 4/15. Sir J. C. & S.

Sheet II

Instructions regarding War Diaries and Intelligence Summaries are contained in F. S. Regs., Part II. and the Staff Manual respectively. Title pages will be prepared in manuscript.

WAR DIARY
290 Brigade R.F.A.
~~INTELLIGENCE~~ SUMMARY.
(Erase heading not required.)

Army Form C. 2118.

Place	Date	Hour	Summary of Events and Information	Remarks and references to Appendices
August	8th	(contd)	transferred to K. 31 c 90. 55.	
"	9th		Barrage fired at 5.30 pm. in conjunction with an infantry attack.	
			B/290 and C/290 moved to more advanced positions in the evening.	
"	10th		Brigade came under the Command of the 4th Australian Divl Artillery.	
			A/290 and D/290 moved to more advanced positions.	
"	11th		Brigade Headquarters moved to K. 27. c. 7.9.	
	13th		Brigade again came under orders of 58th D.A. forming part of the "Liaison Force". All Batteries moved to more forward positions.	
"	20th		The "Liaison Force" ceased to exist and Bde came under Orders of 4 Aus: Div Arty.	
"	22nd		At 4.45 am. Barrage fired in connection with an attack by the 47th Division on the Left.	
"	24th		Barrage fired at 1 am. and BRAY SUR SOMME was captured by Australian Infy. The Batteries moved forward during the day and Headquarters moved to K. 35. a. 6. 3.	
"	25		Barrage fired at 5 am in support of a further attack by the Infantry. Later in the day Batteries moved to positions in	

T2134. Wt. W708—776. 506000. 4/15. Sir J. C. & S.

Sheet III

Instructions regarding War Diaries and Intelligence Summaries are contained in F. S. Regs., Part II. and the Staff Manual respectively. Title pages will be prepared in manuscript.

WAR DIARY or ~~INTELLIGENCE~~ SUMMARY.

290 Brigade R.F.A

(*Erase heading not required.*)

Army Form C. 2118.

Place	Date	Hour	Summary of Events and Information	Remarks and references to Appendices
August	25th	(Cont)	the neighbourhood of BRAY. Headquarters to L 14 a. 8 3.	
			2/Lieut J.M. MASHALL joined to Brigade and was posted to B/290.	
"	27th		All Batteries moved to positions in the neighbourhood of BILLON WOOD. Headquarters being at F. 28. 6. 6 8. Brigade came under orders of the 58th Divl Arty.	
"	28th		At 4.45 am a barrage was fired in conjunction with an attack by the 58th Divisional Infantry.	
"	29th		All Batteries moved forward. Headquarters being established in Quarry in A 30. b 5 3.	
"	30th		All Batteries occupied positions in front of MARRIERS WOOD with Headqrs at B. 27 6. 4 0	
"	31st		At 5.10 am Barrage fired in connection with an attack on MARRIERS WOOD which was taken by our Infantry.	

W.A. Jones. Lt Col
Comdg 290th Brigade R.F.A.

708—776. 500000. 4/15. Sir J. C. & S.

17

290 Bde RFA

Vol 21

Instructions regarding War Diaries and Intelligence Summaries are contained in F. S. Regs., Part II. and the Staff Manual respectively. Title pages will be prepared in manuscript.

WAR DIARY
or
~~INTELLIGENCE SUMMARY.~~
(Erase heading not required.)

Army Form C. 2118.

Place	Date	Hour	Summary of Events and Information	Remarks and references to Appendices
SEPTEMBER	1.		On the night Aug 31/Sept 1st 'A' 'B' & 'D' Batteries moved to more advanced positions. At 5.30 am a barrage was fired in conjunction with an Infantry attack on BOUCHAVESNES, which was captured. In the evening Headquarters and batteries moved forward, coming under orders of the 74th (Yeomanry) Division and performing liaison with the 229 Infantry Brigade.	
	2.		A Barrage was fired at 5.30 am supporting an attack on MOISLAINS. The Infantry took the village, but eventually had to fall back practically to their start line.	
	3		Lieut C.W. Lazenby rejoined the Brigade and was posted to A/290.	
	4		MOISLAINS was found to be evacuated, and positions were reconnoitred W. of the CANAL DU NORD.	
	5		The enemy having withdrawn, the Brigade advanced and bivouacked for the night on the W side of the CANAL DU NORD near MOISLAINS.	
	6.		The Brigade advanced in close support of the Infantry	

Instructions regarding War Diaries and Intelligence Summaries are contained in F. S. Regs., Part II. and the Staff Manual respectively. Title pages will be prepared in manuscript.

WAR DIARY
or
INTELLIGENCE SUMMARY.
(Erase heading not required.)

Army Form C. 2118.

Place	Date	Hour	Summary of Events and Information	Remarks and references to Appendices
			during the day, and in the evening sideslipped north, came under the command of the 58th DA, and occupied positions near GURLU WOOD, liaison being performed with the 175th Infantry Brigade.	
	7		The Batteries again moved forward. Headquarters moved to AIZECOURT-LE-BAS in liaison with the 175th Infantry Brigade. 2/Lt AW Kincook wounded.	
	8		Headquarters moved at 5 am to the North of LIERAMONT, with Headquarters 174th Infantry Brigade. A barrage was fired supporting the attack of this Brigade on EPEHY. The attack was successful, but during the day the Infantry were compelled to withdraw to their original start line.	
	9.		In the afternoon Brigade Headquarters moved to LIERAMONT to act in liaison with the 173rd Infantry Brigade.	
	10		The attack on EPEHY and PEZIERES was resumed, the batteries firing a barrage in support of the 173rd Brigade. The Infantry again captured their objectives, and were again forced	

T2134. Wt. W708—776. 506000. 4/15. Sir J. C. & S.

Instructions regarding War Diaries and Intelligence Summaries are contained in F. S. Regs., Part II. and the Staff Manual respectively. Title pages will be prepared in manuscript.

WAR DIARY
or
INTELLIGENCE SUMMARY.
(Erase heading not required.)

Army Form C. 2118.

Place	Date	Hour	Summary of Events and Information	Remarks and references to Appendices
			back to their start line. 2/Lt. G.C. WOOLVEN went out with an Officers patrol, and failing to find his orderly returning, was presumed a prisoner of war.	
	13		Lt K.A.R. Shattmann joined the Brigade and was posted to C/290.	
	14		New battery positions were reconnoitred E of VILLERS FAUCON and W of EPEHY. The Brigade came under the orders of the 18th DA.	
	17		Headquarters moved to the E of VILLERS FAUCON, batteries to the positions reconnoitred on the 14th.	
	18.		The Brigade supported an attack designed to capture EPEHY, PEZIERES and RONSSOY, and to drive the enemy back on to the Hindenburg line. EPEHY, PEZIERES and RONSSOY were taken but the enemy line remained a short distance W of the Hindenburg Line. 2/Lt. E.V. STALEY was killed, and LIEUT. T. VESEY STRONG was gassed and sent to hospital.	
	19		All batteries moved in the early morning to positions W of RONSSOY. Headquarters were established at St EMILIE	

T2134. Wt. W708—776. 500000. 4/15. Sir J. C. & S.

Army Form C. 2118.

Instructions regarding War Diaries and Intelligence Summaries are contained in F. S. Regs., Part II. and the Staff Manual respectively. Title pages will be prepared in manuscript.

WAR DIARY
or
INTELLIGENCE SUMMARY.
(Erase heading not required.)

Place	Date	Hour	Summary of Events and Information	Remarks and references to Appendices
	20 21 22		Several local attacks made with artillery support but the progress was very slow. Much harassing fire was carried out by day and night.	
	24		'B' Battery was moved 300 yards farther west of RONSSOY, their previous position being constantly and heavily shelled.	
	25		From 10 am the 27th American Division took over the front. The Artillery, under the CRA 4th Australian Division, was reorganised and Lt Col W. A. F. Jones D.S.O. took command of the Centre Group, consisting of the 110th, 290th, & 291st Brigades RFA.	
	26		At 9.30 pm the preparatory 48-hours bombardment for a general attack on the Hindenburg Line began. A special gas concentration fired by 18p	
	27		At 5.30 am the 27th American Division attacked to gain the forming-up line for the main attack. Their objective was gained and prisoners taken, but our infantry by evening were forced back to their original line. Centre Group co-operated. D/290 was heavily shelled in the early morning and 2/Lt. L.F. ROBINSON killed. Wire cutting commenced.	

Instructions regarding War Diaries and Intelligence Summaries are contained in F. S. Regs., Part II. and the Staff Manual respectively. Title pages will be prepared in manuscript.

WAR DIARY
or
INTELLIGENCE SUMMARY.
(Erase heading not required.)

Army Form C. 2118.

Place	Date	Hour	Summary of Events and Information	Remarks and references to Appendices
	28		Positions were reconnoitred E of RONSSOY and occupied at dusk. Brigade Headquarters moved to RONSSOY.	
	29		At 5.30 am the Centre Group fired a creeping barrage supporting the attack of the 27th American Division on the Hindenburg Line. The Hindenburg Line was captured and GOUY and LE CATELET, but during the day there was mixed fighting. The front line at night ran immediately E of the CANAL DE ST QUENTIN.	
	30.		At 1.30 am the 110th, 290th and 291st Brigades came under the command of C.R.A. 3rd Aus. Division. The 110th Brigade RFA left the CENTRE GROUP. The 'Mopping up' of the Hindenburg Line was commenced.	
			The Military Medal was awarded to the following N.C.Os and men. (58th DARO. No. 512 dated 18.9.18)	
			926484 Sergt J.A. LLOYD A/290	
			925579 Sergt A.J. POTTEN B/290	
			97316 Gunner J. TODD C/290	
			237916 Gunner J.A.B.S. STEVENSON C/290	
			925812 Driver H. HODGSON A/290	
			406271 Sapper G. SCOTT-CORMACK R.E. attd. H.Q. 290th Brigade RFA.	

W. H. Jones Lt Col
Cg 290th Bde RFA

D. D. & L., London, E.C.
(A8004) Wt W1771/M2031 750,000 5/17 Sch. 52 Forms/C2118/14

8

Instructions regarding War Diaries and Intelligence Summaries are contained in F. S. Regs., Part II. and the Staff Manual respectively. Title pages will be prepared in manuscript.

WAR DIARY
or
~~INTELLIGENCE SUMMARY.~~
(Erase heading not required.)

6

54 Div
290 Bde RFA
Vol 22

Army Form C. 2118.

Place	Date	Hour	Summary of Events and Information	Remarks and references to Appendices
October.	1st.		Mopping up along the HINDENBURG LINE continued. Artillery re-grouped, the Brigade forming part of the RIGHT GROUP under Lt. Colonel W.G.ALLSOP D.S.O., Commanding 8th Australian Field Artillery Brigade, covering 11th Australian Infantry Brigade.	
	2nd.		Headquarters and Batteries moved to positions W. of BONY.	
	3rd.		At 6.5 a.m. anattack was made under a creeping barrage tp capture the RED LINE including LE CATELET - GOUY - and PROSPECT HILL. These objectives were taken but by the evening the Infantry were forced back to the top of PROSPECT HILL and the Southern portion of LE CATELET and GOUY.	
	4th.		LE CATELET retaken. N.E. portion was lost later under a counter attack.	
	5th.		Headquarters and Batteries moved to N.W. of LE CATELET./ under direct orders of the 113th Infantry Bde, 38th Division. (The Bosch having fallen back during the night).	
	6th.		Headquarters and Batteries moved to positions S. of GOUY re-joining the 18th Divisional Artillery. Headquarters at MONT ST. MARTIN.	
	8th.		Attack was made to capture SERAIN and VILLERS OUTREAUX which was successful. A large number of civilians were released in SERAIN and villages East.	
	9th.		Headquarters and Batteries came out of action and marched to AIZECOURT le BAS Area.	
	11th.		Headquarters and Batteries at intervals marched to TINCOURT and entrained.	
	12/13th.		The Brigade detrained and went into billets at HERSIN coming under Vlllth Corps 1st Army.	
	13h /18th.		Brigade remained at HERSIN.	

18th/

D. D. & L., London, E.C.
(A8004) Wt W1771/M2031 750,000 5/17 Sch. 52 Forms/C2118/14

Army Form C. 2118.

Instructions regarding War Diaries and Intelligence Summaries are contained in F. S. Regs., Part II. and the Staff Manual respectively. Title pages will be prepared in manuscript.

WAR DIARY
or
~~INTELLIGENCE SUMMARY~~.

(Erase heading not required.)

Place	Date	Hour	Summary of Events and Information	Remarks and references to Appendices
October.	18th.		Brigade proceeded by road to HARNES. Coming under the 1st Corps Fifth Army as Divisional Reserve, the Division meeting with little or no opposition in the advance.	
	19th.		Brigade proceeded to RUE DE MONCHEAUX.	
	20th.		Brigade proceeded to VERT BOIS area.	
	21st.		Brigade proceeded to AIX.	
	21/27th.		Brigade remained at AIX in Corps Reserve.	
	27th.		Brigade relieved the 291st Brigade R.F.A. in the Line, coming under orders of the Brigadier General 174th Infantry Brigade, with Brigade Headquarters at RONGY.	
	27/31st.		The Line remained practically stationary on the banks of the SCHELDT being held strongly by the enemy with Machine guns.	

HONOURS AND AWARDS.

THE MILITARY CROSS.

2/Lt. W.T.KING. C/290th Bde. RFA.
2/Lt. L.F.ROBINSON. D/290th Bde. RFA.
(Since Killed in Action).

THE MILITARY MEDAL.

925636. Farr. Sergt. C.F.COOPER. B/290th RFA.
926446. Cpl. Whlr. S.T.TOMLINSON. B/290th RFA.
690181. Driver. A. HOYTON. D/290th RFA.
926265. Driver. C. KERRIDGE. D/290th RFA.

3/.

D. D. & L., London, E.C.
(A8004) Wt W1771/M2031 750,000 5/17 Sch. 52 Forms/C2118/14

Instructions regarding War Diaries and Intelligence Summaries are contained in F. S. Regs., Part II. and the Staff Manual respectively. Title pages will be prepared in manuscript.

WAR DIARY
or
INTELLIGENCE SUMMARY.
(Erase heading not required.)

Army Form C. 2118.

Place	Date	Hour	Summary of Events and Information	Remarks and references to Appendices
			THE MILITARY MEDAL. (Contd).	
			926233. Driver. E. FATHERS. D/290th Bde RFA.	
			690318. Driver. J. ASHCROFT. D/290th Bde RFA.	
			17128. Sergt. H. STAITE. C/290th Bde RFA.	
			925538. Sergt. W.G.BAKER. C/290th Bde RFA.	
			685171. Sergt. J. FORSHAW. B/290th Bde. RFA.	
			191251. Gunner. J. SPENCE. B/290th Bde RFA.	
			W. A. Jones. ....Lt.Colonel. D.S.O. Commanding, 290th BRIGADE R. F. A.	

D. D. & L., London, E.C. (A8004) Wt W1771/M2031 750,000 5/17 Sch. 52 Forms/C2118/14

8

WAR DIARY
or
~~INTELLIGENCE SUMMARY~~.
(Erase heading not required.)

290 Bde RFA
9
Vol 23

Army Form C. 2118.

Instructions regarding War Diaries and Intelligence Summaries are contained in F. S. Regs., Part II. and the Staff Manual respectively. Title pages will be prepared in manuscript.

Place	Date	Hour	Summary of Events and Information	Remarks and references to Appendices
November	1st		The 174th Infantry Brigade with one battalion of the 173rd attached took over the defence of the whole Divisional Front covered by the 290th Brigade with B/242 and D/242 attached under the command of Lt. Colonel W.A.F.JONES D.S.O.	
	1/7th.		Preparations were made for an attack to take place on the Divisional Front on or about the 9th.	
	7/8th.		The enemy retired during the night.	
	9th.		In conjunction with the 174th Infantry Brigade took up the pursuit of the enemy and advanced during the day as far as PONT DE CALLENELLE.	
	10th.		Continued the pursuit as far as BELOEIL receiving a great reception from the civilians in the various villages.	
	11th.		Brigade marched to GROSAGE, news being received just as the Brigade moved off that the Armistice had been signed and that hostilities would cease at 11 a.m.	
	11/17th.		Brigade remained in billets at GROSAGE.	
	14th.		A Thanksgiving Service was held by the 174th Infantry Brigade at which a representative party of the Brigade were present.	
	17th.		Brigade moved to more comfortable billets, Headquarters, B/290 and C/290 being at QUEVAUCAMPS, A/290 and D/290 at BLATON.	
	18/30th.		Brigade remained in billets, the mornings being spent in drill and training, the afternoons in Football and Sports with classes for Education in the evenings.	

<u>HONOURS AND AWARDS.</u>

<u>THE MILITARY CROSS.</u>

Capt.V.BANHAM, C.F. Attd.290th Brigade R.F.A.

J. Eckersley Major for ....Lt.Colonel D.S.O.,
Commanding
290th Brigade R. F. A.

D. D. & L., London, E.C. (A8004) Wt W1771/M2031 750,000 5/17 Sch. 52 Forms/C2118/14

Instructions regarding War Diaries and Intelligence Summaries are contained in F. S. Regs., Part II. and the Staff Manual respectively. Title pages will be prepared in manuscript.

WAR DIARY
or
~~INTELLIGENCE SUMMARY.~~
(Erase heading not required.)

Army Form C. 2118.

December 1918.

Place	Date	Hour	Summary of Events and Information	Remarks and references to Appendices
QUEVAUCAMPS	Dec 1.		Lt. Col. W. A. F. Jones D.S.O. proceeded to ENGLAND on 14 days leave, and a six weeks Senior Officers' Tactical Course at CAMBRIDGE.	
	Dec 2.		The 58th Division was inspected by General Sir H. S. HORNE K.C.B. K.C.M.G. Commanding First Army. The inspection concluded with a march past.	
	Dec 5.		His Majesty King George V visited the Divisional Area, passing through GRANDGLISE and BASECLES. Large numbers of men gathered in groups along the road to cheer His Majesty as he passed.	

J. Sellars [signature]
Major
Cmdg. 290th Brigade RFA.

D. D. & L., London, E.C. (A8004) Wt W1771/M2031 750,000 5/17 Sch. 52 Forms/C2118/14

8

Army Form C. 2118.

58

WAR DIARY
290th - BRIGADE R.F.A.
~~or INTELLIGENCE SUMMARY.~~

(Erase heading not required.)

58 Div

Vol 27

Instructions regarding War Diaries and Intelligence Summaries are contained in F. S. Regs., Part II. and the Staff Manual respectively. Title pages will be prepared in manuscript.

Place	Date	Hour	Summary of Events and Information	Remarks and references to Appendices
MARCH	1919			
QUEVAUCAMPS	8.3.19		Owing to the progress of Demobilisation, the 58th Division was concentrated around LEUZE at the beginning of March. Accordingly QUEVAUCAMPS was evacuated by the 290th Brigade RFA, on the 8th March, Headquarters, 'A' and 'D' Batteries moving to BLICQUY, 'B' and 'C' Batteries to AUBECHIES. Demobilisation proceeded during the month.	

W. A. Jones
Lieutenant Colonel.
Commanding
290th Brigade R.F.A.

D. D. & L., London, E.C. (A8204) Wt W1771/M2031 750,000 5/17 Sch. 52 Forms/C2118/14

www.ingramcontent.com/pod-product-compliance
Lightning Source LLC
Chambersburg PA
CBHW081452160426
43193CB00013B/2453